cocktails

cocktails

First published in the U.K. in 1999 by Hamlyn for WHSmith, Greenbridge Road, Swindon SN3 3LD

Octopus Publishing Group Limited
2–4 Heron Quays
London E14 4JP

ISBN 0600 60452 7

Printed in China

Notes

1 Standard level spoon measurements are used in all recipes.

1 tablespoon = one 15 ml spoon
1 teaspoon = one 5 ml spoon

2 Both imperial and metric measurements have been given where applicable. Use one set of measurements only and not a mixture of both.

3 Eggs should be medium unless otherwise stated. The Department of Health advises that eggs should not be consumed raw. This book contains drinks made with uncooked eggs. It is prudent for more vulnerable people, such as pregnant and nursing mothers, invalids and the elderly, to avoid these drinks.

4 Milk should be full fat unless otherwise stated.

5 The measure that has been used in the cocktail recipes is based on a bar jigger, which is 45 ml(1½ fl oz). If preferred, a different volume can be used providing the proportions are kept constant within a drink and suitable adjustments are made to spoon measurements, where they occur.

contents

introduction

Cocktails are pure escapism. Short mixed drinks – usually spirit-based – they are made to an exact recipe rather than poured in a haphazard fashion, one of the reasons for their deceptively powerful kick. They can also, though this is a very modern trend, be non-alcoholic.

Despite their association with the bright young things of the 1920s, cocktails have been around for a long time. Mixed drinks were popular in the nineteenth century, and the use of the word cocktail goes back to 1806, or 1809, depending which reference book you prefer. Daisies, cobblers and fixes, for example, are all part of Victorian drinking history, while punch goes back even further, to the 18th century. As well as having their own bar equipment and glasses, cocktails have their own language. Among the best-known names, a cobbler is a wine-based mixed drink, originally made with sherry; sours are mixtures of spirit, lemon and sugar, and daisies are similar to sours but with the addition of a sweet syrup.

Juleps, long drinks made with bourbon whiskey and mint, are part of the history of the Deep South, and it is impossible to enjoy a really well made julep without succumbing to fantasies of a lifestyle with overtones of *Gone With the Wind*. (Captain Marryat (1792–1848), better known for his adventure stories such as *Mr Midshipman Easy* and *The Children of the New Forest*, felt that mint juleps were the perfect drink for when the temperature was 100°F but grudgingly conceded that they were still enjoyable at 70°F!) The Collinses (see page 37) are another American drink, while slings, sweetish long drinks which are usually with a gin base, are associated with colonial life in the Far East. Egg nogs have long been popular on both sides of the Atlantic, and are traditionally served at Christmas.

The word punch is said to come from *panch*, the Hindustani word for five, and to refer to the five elements in punch (spirit, citrus, sugar, spice and water). However, the classic formula for a rum punch in the West Indies 'One of sour, two of sweet, three of strong and four of weak' – contains only four elements, being made without spice. (The sour element is a lime slice, the sweet is syrup, the strong is rum and the weak is water.)

Glasses

There is no reason why many cocktails shouldn't be served in a standard wine glass, which holds 150 ml (5 fl oz). However, there is no doubt that using the classic vee-shaped cocktail glass or the curiously shaped Margarita glass adds to the pleasure of the occasion; old-fashioned glasses are convenient for a short drink on the rocks, while for longer drinks a highball glass, a hurricane glass or the even taller Collins glass are most suitable. Hot punches should be served in a mug or a heatproof glass with a handle.

Bar Equipment

The basic pieces of bar equipment for the serious drinks maker are a cocktail shaker, a mixing glass and a blender. The shaker, which usually comes with a built-in strainer, is for drinks that contain ingredients such as eggs, cream, thick liqueurs and slices or chunks of fruit which need a really thorough shake to blend all the elements. The mixing glass (actually large enough to contain several drinks) is for drinks that are just stirred together. It is used in conjunction with a bar spoon and then strained or poured directly into glasses. The blender is for smoothies and other drinks with ice cream and fruit.

A set of bar measures ensures absolute accuracy and saves a lot of time, and a coil-rimmed bar strainer is also helpful. Other important pieces of bar equipment, most of which will be found in any kitchen, are a lemon squeezer, a paring knife and chopping board, ice trays and ice containers, teaspoons and tablespoons and of course corkscrews and bottle openers, tea towels and cocktail sticks. A waiter's friend is a useful gadget to have on hand in case corks prove stubborn. Teaspoons and tablespoons should be kept in a jug of water when not in use so that they are rinsed between mixes.

Ice

Ice is essential for a well-made cocktail, so always make sure that you have plenty available when you are making drinks. When ice is added to a shaker, it acts as a beater as well as cooling the mixture. Use tongs rather than a spoon for putting ice into drinks, so that you don't add cold water with the ice cubes. Sometimes recipes ask for cracked ice or crushed ice. To make cracked ice put a handful of ice cubes into a strong polythene bag and hit it with a rolling pin. For crushed ice, simply go on hitting the ice for a little longer.

Sugar Syrup

Sugar syrup is used in many cocktails as it is easier to stir into cold drinks than sugar. To make up a supply, combine equal quantites of caster sugar and water (say 6 tablespoons of each) and bring them to the boil in a small saucepan, stirring until the sugar is dissolved, then boil for 1 minute without stirring. Sugar syrup can be stored in a sterilized bottle in the refrigerator for up to 2 months.

'Let's get out of these wet clothes and into a dry Martini.'

Alexander Woollcott

Decorating Cocktails

A cocktail looks good with a decorative finish. Traditional decorations include slices of lemon, orange, lime or cucumber, twists of citrus rind, cocktail cherries and green olives. Herbs, especially mint, add flavour as well as looking attractive. Long thin spirals of lemon or orange rind are an up-to-date touch as are strawberries, whole or halved, and other pieces of fruit, including pineapple and mango. Glass swizzle sticks and tiny paper parasols make an attractive finishing touch and can save you time if you are mixing drinks on your own. Ice cubes frozen with sprigs of herbs, again mint is a favourite, or raspberries look most attractive and can be prepared well ahead to save time.

dry martini •

burnsides •

sapphire martini •

salty dog •

morning glory fizz •

gin sling •

ben's orange cream •

lime gin fizz •

clover club •

pink clover club •

gin cup •

alice springs •

maiden's prayer •

knockout •

gin: mother's ruin

dry martini

Put the ice cubes into a mixing glass. Pour the vermouth and gin over the ice and stir (never shake) vigorously and evenly without splashing, then strain into a chilled cocktail glass. Serve with a green olive and a straw.

Pictured Left

5–6 ice cubes

½ measure dry vermouth

3 measures gin

1 green olive

Serves 1
Preparation time: 3 minutes

The Dry Martini, which was invented at the Knickerbocker Hotel in New York in 1910, has become the most famous cocktail of all. Lemon rind is sometimes used as a decoration instead of a green olive.

burnsides

Put 4–5 ice cubes into a cocktail shaker. Dash the bitters over the ice, add the cherry brandy, sweet and dry vermouths and gin. Shake lightly, then strain into a glass over the remaining ice cubes. Decorate with lemon rind strips.

Pictured Right

8–10 ice cubes

2 drops Angostura bitters

1 teaspoon cherry brandy

1 measure sweet vermouth

2 measures dry vermouth

2 measures gin

lemon rind strips

Serves 1
Preparation time: 3 minutes

sapphire martini

Put the ice cubes into a cocktail shaker. Pour in the gin and blue Curaçao and shake well to mix. Strain into a chilled cocktail glass and carefully drop in a cocktail cherry, if using.

4–5 ice cubes

2 measures gin

½ measure blue Curaçao

1 blue cocktail cherry (optional)

Serves 1

Preparation time: 2 minutes

A Salty Dog can also be made with vodka. Sometimes the glass is rimmed with salt, like a Margarita.

2–3 ice cubes
pinch of salt
1 measure gin
2–2½ measures fresh grapefruit juice
orange slice, to decorate

Serves 1

Preparation time: 2 minutes

Put the ice cubes into an old fashioned glass. Put the salt on the ice and add the gin and grapefruit juice. Stir gently and serve. Decorate with an orange slice.

salty dog

16

morning glory fizz

Put the ice cubes into a cocktail shaker. Pour the lemon juice, sugar syrup and gin over the ice. Add the egg white, then the pernod and shake until a frost forms. Strain into a chilled old fashioned glass, top up with ginger ale and serve with a straw.

4–5 ice cubes

1 measure fresh lemon juice

½ teaspoon sugar syrup

3 measures gin

1 egg white

3 drops pernod

ginger ale

Serves 1
Preparation time: 4 minutes

4–5 ice cubes
juice of ½ lemon
1 measure cherry brandy
3 measures gin
soda water
cherries, to decorate (optional)

Serves 1
Preparation time: 3 minutes

Put the ice cubes into a cocktail shaker. Pour the lemon juice, cherry brandy and gin over the ice and shake until a frost forms. Pour without straining into a hurricane glass and top up with soda water. Decorate with cherries, if liked, and serve with straws.

gin sling

ben's orange cream

Put the ice cubes into a cocktail shaker. Pour the Cointreau, cream and gin over the ice. Add the sugar syrup to the gin mixture and shake until a frost forms. Pour into a large glass and decorate with a chocolate flake.

Pictured Left

4–5 ice cubes
1 measure Cointreau
1 measure single cream
3 measures gin
1 tablespoon sugar syrup
chocolate flake, to decorate

Serves 1

Preparation time: 4 minutes

lime gin fizz

Put the ice cubes into a tall glass. Pour the gin and the lime cordial over the ice cubes. Top up with soda water, decorate with wedges of lime and serve with straws.

Pictured Right

4–5 ice cubes
2 measures gin
1 measure lime cordial
soda water
lime wedges, to decorate

Serves 1

Preparation time: 3 minutes

clover club

Put the ice cubes into a cocktail shaker. Pour the lime juice, sugar syrup, egg white and gin over the ice and shake until a frost forms. Strain into a tumbler and serve decorated with grated lime rind and a lime wedge.

4–5 ice cubes

juice of 1 lime

½ teaspoon sugar syrup

1 egg white

3 measures gin

To Decorate:

grated lime rind

lime wedge

Serves 1
Preparation time: 3 minutes

4–5 ice cubes
juice of 1 lime
dash of grenadine
1 egg white
3 measures gin
strawberry slice, to decorate

Put the ice cubes into a cocktail shaker. Pour the lime juice, grenadine, egg white and gin over the ice. Shake until a frost forms, then strain into a cocktail glass. Decorate with a strawberry slice and serve with a straw.

Serves 1

Preparation time: 3 minutes

pink clover club

Grenadine is a sweet non-alcoholic syrup made from pomegranates, which give it its rich rosy pink colour.

gin cup

Put the mint and sugar syrup into an old fashioned glass and stir them about to bruise the mint slightly. Fill the glass with chopped ice, add the lemon juice and gin and stir until a frost begins to form. Decorate with extra mint sprigs.

3 mint sprigs, extra to decorate

1 teaspoon sugar syrup

chopped ice

juice of ½ lemon

3 measures gin

Serves 1

Preparation time: 4 minutes

4–5 ice cubes
1 measure fresh lemon juice
1 measure fresh orange juice
½ teaspoon grenadine
3 measures gin
3 drops Angostura bitters
soda water
orange slice, to decorate

Serves 1

Preparation time: 4 minutes

Put the ice cubes into a cocktail shaker. Pour in the lemon juice, orange juice, grenadine and gin. Add the bitters and shake until a frost forms. Pour into a tall glass and top up with soda water. Decorate with a slice of orange and serve with straws.

alice springs

maiden's prayer

Put the ice cubes into a cocktail shaker. Pour the bitters over the ice, add the lemon juice, Cointreau and gin and shake until a frost forms. Strain into a cocktail glass and serve with a straw.

Pictured Left

4–5 ice cubes
3 drops Angostura bitters
juice of 1 lemon
1 measure Cointreau
2 measures gin

Serves 1

Preparation time: 4 minutes

knockout

Put the ice cubes into a mixing glass. Pour the vermouth, crème de menthe and gin over the ice, stir vigorously, then strain into a chilled old fashioned glass. Add the pernod and serve with a lemon slice.

Pictured Right

4–5 ice cubes
1 measure dry vermouth
½ measure white crème de menthe
2 measures gin
1 drop pernod
lemon slice, to serve

Serves 1

Preparation time: 4 minutes

Crème de menthe is a sweetish mint-flavoured liqueur, which may be green or white in colour, although the flavour remains the same. The white version is used here to blend with the milky colour of the pernod.

27

whisky milk punch •

golden daisy •

southerly buster •

scots guards •

tar •

bunny hug •

suburban •

algonquin •

skipper •

mike collins •

clear skies ahead •

walters •

virginia mint julep •

mississippi punch •

whisky: the hard stuff

whisky milk punch

Put the ice cubes into a cocktail shaker. Pour the sugar syrup, whisky and milk over the ice and shake until a frost forms. Pour without straining into an old fashioned glass, sprinkle with grated nutmeg and serve.

Pictured Left

4–5 ice cubes
1 teaspoon sugar syrup
2 measures whisky
3 measures milk
grated nutmeg

Serves 1

Preparation time: 3 minutes

golden daisy

Put the ice cubes into a cocktail shaker. Pour the lemon juice, sugar syrup, Cointreau and whisky over the ice and shake vigorously until a frost forms. Strain into an old fashioned glass and serve decorated with a lime wedge.

Pictured Right

4–5 ice cubes
juice of 1 lemon
1 teaspoon sugar syrup
½ measure Cointreau
3 measures whisky
lime wedge, to decorate

Serves 1

Preparation time: 3 minutes

This is one of the drinks that date back to the nineteenth century but seem surprisingly modern. Although daisies may also be made with gin or rum, the general feeling is that whisky, especially bourbon, makes the best drink.

southerly buster

Put the ice cubes into a mixing glass. Pour the Curaçao and whisky over the ice, stir vigorously, then strain into a chilled cocktail glass. Twist the lemon rind over the drink and drop it in. Serve with a straw.

4–5 ice cubes

1 measure blue Curaçao

3 measures whisky

1 piece of lemon rind

Serves 1

Preparation time: 3 minutes

4–5 ice cubes
juice of 1 lemon
juice of ½ orange
½ teaspoon grenadine
3 measures whisky

Serves 1
Preparation time: 4 minutes

Put the ice cubes into a mixing glass. Pour the lemon juice, orange juice, grenadine and whisky over the ice. Stir vigorously, then strain into a chilled cocktail glass. Serve with a straw.

scots guards

tar

Put the ice cubes into a cocktail shaker. Pour in the lemon juice, grenadine, crème de cacao and whisky. Shake until a frost forms, then strain into a chilled cocktail glass. Serve with a straw.

Pictured Left

4–5 ice cubes
juice of 1 lemon
½ teaspoon grenadine
1 measure crème de cacao
3 measures whisky

Serves 1

Preparation time: 3 minutes

Crème de cacao is a chocolate liqueur available in a colourless version as well as a chocolate-coloured one.

bunny hug

Put the ice cubes into a mixing glass. Pour the pernod, gin and whisky over the ice, stir vigorously, then strain into a chilled cocktail glass. Serve with a straw.

Pictured Right

4–5 ice cubes
1 measure pernod
1 measure gin
3 measures whisky

Serves 1

Preparation time: 2 minutes

suburban

Put the ice cubes into a mixing glass. Shake the bitters over the ice then pour in the port, rum and whisky. Stir vigorously, then pour into a chilled old fashioned glass.

4–5 ice cubes

3 drops orange bitters or Angostura bitters

1 measure port

1 measure dark rum

3 measures bourbon or Scotch whisky

Serves 1

Preparation time: 3 minutes

This cocktail takes its name from the Algonquin Hotel in New York, made famous by Dorothy Parker, James Thurber and the other writers and artists of the *New Yorker* magazine.

algonquin

4–5 ice cubes

1 measure unsweetened pineapple juice

1 measure dry vermouth

3 measures bourbon or Scotch whisky

Put the ice cubes into a mixing glass. Pour the pineapple juice, vermouth and whisky over the ice. Stir vigorously, until nearly frothy, then strain into a chilled cocktail glass. Serve decorated with a cocktail parasol and drink with a straw.

Serves 1

Preparation time: 3 minutes

skipper

Put the ice cubes into a mixing glass. Pour the grenadine over the ice and add the orange juice, vermouth and whisky. Stir vigorously, until nearly frothy, then pour into a tumbler. Decorate with an orange slice and serve with a straw.

4–5 ice cubes

4 drops grenadine

juice of ½ orange

1 measure dry vermouth

3 measures rye or Scotch whisky

orange wedge, to decorate

Serves 1

Preparation time: 3 minutes

The Collins is the longest and most refreshing of drinks – and there are Collinses made with just about every spirit. The John Collins is made with gin (in the USA it is called a Tom Collins), Sandy Collins is made with Scotch whisky and Pierre Collins with brandy. The Rum Collins is made with dark rum and the Pedro Collins with white rum, while a Collins made with vodka is simply known as a Vodka Collins.

5–6 ice cubes
juice of 1 lemon
1 tablespoon sugar syrup
3 measures Irish whiskey
1 orange slice
1 cocktail cherry
soda water
orange rind spiral, to decorate

Put the ice cubes into a cocktail shaker. Pour the lemon juice, sugar syrup and whiskey over the ice and shake until a frost forms. Pour without straining into a tumbler or Collins glass and add the orange slice and cocktail cherry speared on a cocktail stick. Top up with the soda water, stir lightly and serve decorated with an orange rind spiral.

Serves 1

Preparation time: 4 minutes

mike collins

clear skies ahead

Put the ice cubes into a cocktail shaker. Pour in the sugar syrup, lemon juice, grenadine, egg white and whisky. Shake until a frost forms, then pour into an old fashioned glass. Serve decorated with a cocktail parasol.

Pictured Left

4–5 ice cubes

½ teaspoon sugar syrup

juice of ½ lemon

½ teaspoon grenadine

1 egg white

2 measures whisky

Serves 1

Preparation time: 3 minutes

walters

Put the ice cubes into a mixing glass. Pour the lemon juice, orange juice and whisky over the ice. Stir vigorously, then strain into a chilled old fashioned glass. Serve decorated with an orange slice. Drink with a straw.

Pictured Right

4–5 ice cubes

juice of ½ lemon

juice of ½ orange

3 measures bourbon or Scotch whisky

orange slice, to decorate

Serves 1

Preparation time: 4 minutes

virginia mint julep

Put the mint sprigs into an iced silver mug or tall glass. Add the sugar syrup, then crush the mint into the syrup with a teaspoon. Fill the mug or a glass with dry crushed ice, pour the whiskey over the ice and stir gently. Pack in more crushed ice and stir until a frost forms. Wrap the mug or glass in a table napkin and serve decorated with a mint sprig.

9 tender young mint sprigs, extra to decorate

1 teaspoon sugar syrup

crushed ice

3 measures bourbon whiskey

Serves 1

Preparation time: 5 minutes

Making the perfect julep is a time-consuming business. Ideally it should be served in a silver mug which must be thoroughly chilled, if not iced. Second, only crushed ice that has been pounded and dried as much as possible should be used. Third, the mug mustn't be touched during the preparation otherwise the frost will disappear. If you haven't got a silver mug, use a tall glass instead.

crushed ice
3 drops Angostura bitters
1 teaspoon sugar syrup
juice of 1 lemon
1 measure brandy
1 measure dark rum
2 measures whisky

Half-fill a tall glass with crushed ice. Shake the bitters over the ice. Pour in the sugar syrup and the lemon juice, then stir gently to mix thoroughly. Add the brandy, rum and whisky, in that order, stir once and serve with straws.

Serves 1

Preparation time: 3 minutes

mississippi punch

rum: kill-devil

½ lime

2 measures pineapple juice

1 measure white rum

1 teaspoon sugar

3–4 ice cubes

ginger ale

lime slice, to decorate

Cut the lime into 4 pieces, put them into a blender or food processor with the pineapple juice, rum and sugar and blend until smooth. Put the ice into a hurricane glass or large goblet, pour in the drink and top up with ginger ale. Decorate with the lime slice and serve with straws.

Serves 1
Preparation time: 4 minutes

havana beach

batiste

Put the ice cubes into a mixing glass. Pour the Grand Marnier and rum over the ice, stir vigorously then strain into a cocktail glass.

4–5 ice cubes

1 measure Grand Marnier

2 measures golden or dark rum

Serves 1
Preparation time: 3 minutes

Grand Marnier is a brandy-based orange liqueur. It is made by a French liqueur company hence its presence in this cocktail from one of the French speaking islands in the Caribbean.

pink rum

Shake the bitters into a highball glass and swirl them around. Add the ice cubes, then pour in the rum, cranberry juice and soda water and serve decorated with a lime slice.

Pictured Left

3 drops Angostura bitters

3–4 ice cubes

2 measures white rum

2 measures cranberry juice

1 measure soda water

lime slice, to decorate

Serves 1
Preparation time: 4 minutes

zombie christophe

Put the ice cubes into a mixing glass. Pour the lime or lemon juice, orange juice, pineapple juice, Curaçao, white and golden rums over the ice. Stir vigorously, then pour without straining into a tumbler. Top with the dark rum, stir gently and serve decorated with a lemon slice and a mint sprig.

Pictured Right

4–5 ice cubes

juice of 1 lime or lemon

juice of ½ orange

250 ml (8 fl oz) unsweetened pineapple juice

1 measure blue Curaçao

1 measure white rum

1 measure golden rum

½ measure dark rum

To Decorate:

lime or lemon slice

mint sprig

Serves 1
Preparation time: 5 minutes

grenada

Put the ice cubes into a mixing glass. Pour the orange juice, vermouth and rum over the ice. Stir vigorously then strain into a chilled cocktail glass. Sprinkle a little ground cinnamon on top and serve.

4–5 ice cubes

juice of ½ orange

1 measure sweet vermouth

3 measures golden or dark rum

ground cinnamon

Serves 1

Preparation time: 4 minutes

Zombies contain all three types of rum - dark, golden and white. The darker rums are aged in charred oak casks while white rums are aged in stainless steel tanks.

crushed ice
juice of 1 lemon
juice of 1 orange
juice of ½ grapefruit
3 drops Angostura bitters
1 teaspoon soft brown sugar
1 measure white rum
1 measure golden rum
1 measure dark rum

To Decorate:
lime slices
orange slices

Serves 1
Preparation time: 6 minutes

Put the crushed ice into a mixing glass. Pour the lemon, orange and grapefruit juices over the ice and splash in the bitters. Add the sugar and pour in the three rums. Stir vigorously then pour without straining into a Collins glass. Decorate with lime and orange slices.

zombie prince

tobago fizz

Put the ice cubes into a cocktail shaker. Pour the lime or lemon juice, orange juice, rum, cream and sugar syrup over the ice. Shake until a frost forms then strain into a goblet. Top with soda water and serve decorated with an orange slice and a strawberry slice on a cocktail stick and drink with straws.

4–5 ice cubes
juice of ½ lime or lemon
juice of ½ orange
3 measures golden rum
1 measure single cream
½ teaspoon sugar syrup
soda water

To Decorate:
orange slice
strawberry slice

Serves 1

Preparation time: 5 minutes

4–5 ice cubes
3 drops Angostura bitters
juice of ½ lime
1 teaspoon Curaçao or blue Curaçao
1 teaspoon sugar syrup
3 measures golden or dark rum
lime slices, to decorate

Serves 1
Preparation time: 4 minutes

Put the ice cubes into a cocktail shaker. Shake the bitters over the ice. Pour in the lime juice, Curaçao, sugar syrup and rum and shake until a frost forms. Strain into an old fashioned glass. Decorate with lime slices.

discovery bay

Curaçao comes from the Dutch Caribbean island of that name. It is produced in several colours including a vivid blue, but whatever the colour it is always orange flavoured.

daiquiri

Put lots of cracked ice into a cocktail shaker. Pour the lime juice, sugar syrup and rum over the ice. Shake thoroughly until a frost forms then strain into a chilled cocktail glass.

cracked ice
juice of 2 limes
1 teaspoon sugar syrup
3 measures white rum

Serves 1
Preparation time: 4 minutes

The Daiquiri was created by an American mining engineer working in Cuba in 1896. He was expecting VIP guests and his supplies of gin had run out so he extemporized with rum – and created this classic cocktail.

1 measure white rum

½ measure crème de fraises

½ measure fresh lemon juice

4 ripe strawberries, hulled

crushed ice

To Decorate:

strawberry slice

mint sprig

Serves 1
Preparation time: 5 minutes

Put the rum, crème de fraises, lemon juice, strawberries and ice into a food processor or blender and process at a slow speed for 5 seconds, then at high speed for about 20 seconds. Pour into a chilled glass and decorate with a strawberry slice and a mint sprig.

strawberry daiquiri

punch julien

Pour the lime juice and pineapple juice into a mixing glass and dash in the bitters. Pour in the grenadine and golden and dark rums and add the fruit. Stir thoroughly then chill in the refrigerator for 3 hours. Fill an old fashioned glass with cracked ice. Pour the punch over the ice and add the fruit. Sprinkle with nutmeg and serve decorated with a pineapple wedge.

Pictured Left

juice of 2 limes

1 measure unsweetened pineapple juice

3 drops Angostura bitters

½ teaspoon grenadine

1 measure golden rum

3 measures dark rum

1 lime slice

1 lemon slice

1 orange slice

1 pineapple wedge, extra to decorate

cracked ice

grated nutmeg

Serves 1

Preparation time: 6 minutes, plus chilling

bahamas punch

Pour the lemon juice and sugar syrup into a mixing glass. Shake in the bitters, then add the grenadine, rum and orange and lemon slices. Stir thoroughly and chill in the refrigerator for 3 hours. To serve, fill an old fashioned glass with cracked ice, pour in the punch without straining and sprinkle with nutmeg.

Pictured Right

juice of 1 lemon

1 teaspoon sugar syrup

3 drops Angostura bitters

½ teaspoon grenadine

3 measures golden or white rum

1 orange slice

1 lemon slice

cracked ice

grated nutmeg

Serves 1

Preparation time: 5 minutes, plus chilling

brandy: eau-de-vie -de-vin

brandy manhattan

Put the ice cubes into a mixing glass. Pour the vermouth and brandy over the ice and stir vigorously. Pour into a chilled glass and decorate with the cocktail cherry.

4–5 ice cubes

1 measure sweet vermouth

3 measures brandy

1 cocktail cherry, to decorate

Serves 1

Preparation time: 3 minutes

This cocktail dates back to the First World War. It was made for a man who travelled to a Paris bar in a chauffeur-driven motorcycle sidecar.

4–5 ice cubes
juice of 1 lemon
1 measure Cointreau
2 measures brandy

To Decorate:
orange rind
cocktail cherry

Serves 1
Preparation time: 3 minutes

Put the ice cubes into a mixing glass. Pour the lemon juice, Cointreau and brandy over the ice and stir vigorously. Strain into a chilled cocktail glass. Decorate with orange rind and a cocktail cherry on a cocktail stick.

brandy sidecar

brandy classic

Put the ice cubes into a cocktail shaker. Pour in the brandy, Curaçao maraschino liqueur and lemon juice and shake together. Strain into a chilled cocktail glass. Add some cracked ice and a wedge of lemon and serve.

4–5 ice cubes
1 measure brandy
1 measure blue Curaçao
1 measure maraschino liqueur
juice of ½ lemon
cracked ice
lemon wedge, to serve

Serves 1

Preparation time: 3 minutes

Maraschino liqueur is a sweet cherry brandy made in Italy. Substitute another type of cherry brandy if you cannot find it.

crushed ice

1 teaspoon sugar syrup

juice of ½ lemon

½ measure cherry brandy

1 measure brandy

lemon slice, to serve

Half-fill a tumbler with crushed ice. Add the sugar syrup, lemon juice, cherry brandy and brandy and stir. Serve with a slice of lemon.

Serves 1
Preparation time: 3 minutes

brandy fix

paradise

Put the ice cubes into a cocktail shaker. Add the lemon juice, orange juice, gin and apricot brandy and shake together. Strain into a chilled cocktail glass and decorate with slices of lemon and orange.

Pictured Left

4–5 ice cubes

1 dash fresh lemon juice

1 measure fresh orange juice

1 measure gin

1 measure apricot brandy

To Decorate:

lemon slice

orange slice

Serves 1
Preparation time: 4 minutes

heir apparent

Put the ice cubes into a mixing glass. Shake the bitters over the ice and pour in the brandy. Stir vigorously, then strain into a chilled cocktail glass. Add the crème de menthe and serve decorated with the mint sprig.

Pictured Right

4–5 ice cubes

3 drops orange bitters or Angostura bitters

3 measures brandy

3 drops white crème de menthe

mint sprig, to decorate

Serves 1
Preparation time: 3 minutes

egg nog

Half-fill a cocktail shaker with ice. Add the egg, sugar syrup, brandy and milk and shake well for about 1 minute. Strain into a tumbler and sprinkle with some grated nutmeg. Drink with a straw, if liked.

4–5 ice cubes

1 egg

1 tablespoon sugar syrup

2 measures brandy

150 ml (¼ pint) milk

grated nutmeg, to decorate

Serves 1

Preparation time: 4 minutes

Although egg nogs have a deceptively mild appearance, they are very potent, the Baltimore version in particular, so approach them with caution!

4–5 ice cubes
1 egg
1 tablespoon sugar syrup
½ measure brandy
½ measure dark rum
½ measure Madeira
2 measures milk

To Decorate:
ground cinnamon
cinnamon stick

Half-fill a cocktail shaker with ice cubes. Add the egg, sugar syrup, brandy, rum, Madeira and milk and shake well for about 1 minute. Strain into a goblet and sprinkle with cinnamon. Serve with a cinnamon stick.

Serves 1
Preparation time: 4 minutes

baltimore egg nog

brandy sour

Put the ice cubes into a cocktail shaker. Shake the bitters over the ice, add the lemon juice, brandy and sugar syrup and shake until a frost forms. Strain into a tumbler and decorate with lemon slices on a cocktail stick. Serve with a straw.

4–5 ice cubes
3 drops Angostura bitters
juice of 1 lemon
3 measures brandy
1 teaspoon sugar syrup
lemon slices, to decorate

Serves 1

Preparation time: 4 minutes

east india

Put the ice cubes into a mixing glass. Shake the bitters over the ice and add the pineapple juice, Curaçao and brandy. Stir until frothy, then strain into a chilled cocktail glass. Decorate with a spiral of orange rind tied into a knot.

4–5 ice cubes

3 drops Angostura bitters

½ measure pineapple juice

½ measure blue Curaçao

2 measures brandy

orange rind, to decorate

Serves 1

Preparation time: 3 minutes

brandy cuban

Place the ice cubes in a tumbler and pour over the brandy and lime juice. Stir to mix. Top up with cola and decorate with a lime slice. Drink through a straw.

2–3 ice cubes
1½ measures brandy
juice of ½ lime
cola
lime slice, to decorate

Serves 1

Preparation time: 3 minutes

This cocktail is named after Bobby Jones, the American golfer whose heyday was in the 1920s and '30s. He is regarded as the greatest amateur player of all time.

- 4–5 ice cubes
- juice of 1 lemon
- ½ teaspoon grenadine
- 1 measure crème de cacao
- 3 measures brandy

Serves 1
Preparation time: 3 minutes

Put the ice cubes into a cocktail shaker. Pour the lemon juice, grenadine, crème de cacao and brandy over the ice and shake until a frost forms. Strain into a tumbler and serve with a straw.

bobby jones

monte rosa

Put the ice cubes into a mixing glass. Pour the lime juice, Cointreau and brandy over the ice and stir vigorously. Strain into a chilled cocktail glass.

Pictured Left

4–5 ice cubes

juice of ½ lime

1 measure Cointreau

3 measures brandy

Serves 1

Preparation time: 3 minutes

coffee flip

Put 4–5 ice cubes into a cocktail shaker. Pour in the brandy, Kahlúa, cream, and sugar syrup then add the egg, coffee and milk and shake well for 45 seconds. Put the remaining ice cubes into a tall glass, strain the drink over the ice and sprinkle with ground coriander.

Pictured Right

8–10 ice cubes

1 measure brandy

1 measure Kahlúa

2 teaspoons double cream

1½ teaspoons sugar syrup

1 egg, beaten

½ teaspoon instant coffee

125 ml (4 fl oz) milk

ground coriander, to decorate

Serves 1

Preparation time: 4 minutes

Kahlúa is a coffee-based liqueur from Mexico. Among its other flavourings are vanilla and herbs.

vodka: zhizennia voda

vodka sazerac

Put the sugar cube into an old fashioned glass and shake the bitters on to it. Add the pernod to the glass and swirl it about so that it clings to the side of the glass. Drop in the ice cubes and pour in the vodka. Top up with lemonade then stir gently and serve.

1 sugar cube
2 drops Angostura bitters
3 drops pernod
2–3 ice cubes
2 measures vodka
lemonade

Serves 1

Preparation time: 4 minutes

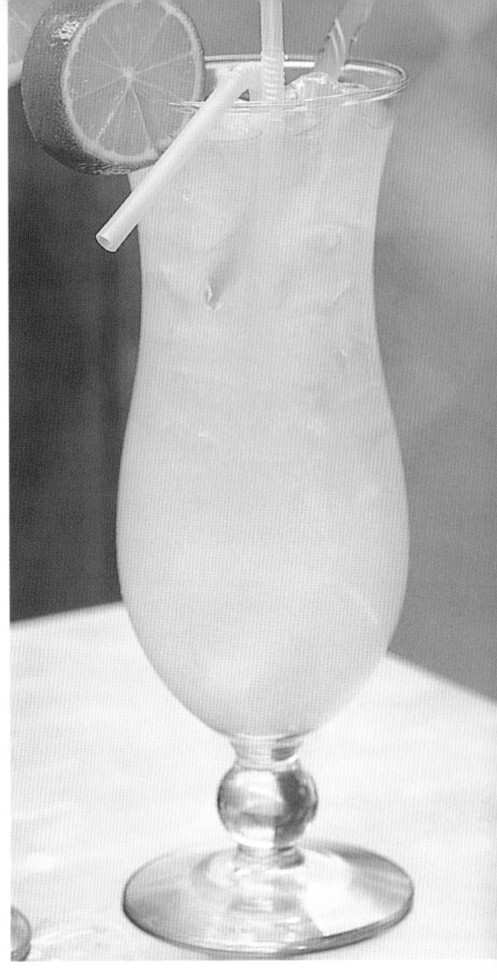

This drink is one of those happy accidents. It was invented in 1941 by an employee of a US drinks firm in conjunction with a Los Angeles bar owner who was overstocked with ginger beer. It was originally served in a copper mug.

3–4 cracked ice cubes
2 measures vodka
juice of 2 limes
ginger beer
lime and orange slices, to decorate

Serves 1
Preparation time: 4 minutes

Put the cracked ice into a cocktail shaker. Add the vodka and lime juice and shake well. Pour into a hurricane glass, top up with ginger beer and stir gently. Decorate with lime and orange slices and serve with straws.

moscow mule

vodka martini

Put the ice cubes into a mixing glass. Pour the vermouth and vodka over the ice and stir vigorously, without splashing. Strain into a chilled cocktail glass, drop in the olive and serve.

4–5 ice cubes

¼ measure dry vermouth

3 measures vodka

1 green olive

Serves 1

Preparation time: 3 minutes

This is one of those drinks which have changed considerably over the years. In the 1930s it was made with gin rather than vodka and with grenadine and lemon juice instead of cranberry juice and grapefruit juice.

1 measure vodka
1½ measures cranberry juice
1½ measures fresh grapefruit juice
5 ice cubes, crushed
lime slice, to decorate

Put the vodka, cranberry juice and grapefruit juice into a tall glass with the ice cubes and stir well. Decorate with a lime slice and drink through a straw.

Serves 1

Preparation time: 3 minutes

sea breeze

vodka twister fizz

Put the ice cubes into a cocktail shaker. Pour the lemon juice, sugar syrup, egg white, pernod and vodka over the ice and shake until a frost forms. Pour without straining into a highball glass and top up with ginger ale. Stir once or twice, decorate with a lime slice and serve.

Pictured Left

4–5 ice cubes
juice of 1 lemon
½ teaspoon sugar syrup
1 egg white
3 drops pernod
3 measures vodka
ginger ale
lime slice, to decorate

Serves 1

Preparation time: 4 minutes

down-under fizz

Put the ice cubes into a cocktail shaker. Pour the lemon and orange juices, grenadine and vodka over the ice and shake until a frost forms. Pour without straining into a Collins glass and top with soda water. Serve with a straw.

Pictured Right

4–5 ice cubes
juice of 1 lemon
juice of ½ orange
½ teaspoon grenadine
3 measures vodka
soda water

Serves 1

Preparation time: 3 minutes

harvey wallbanger

Put half the ice cubes, the vodka and orange juice into a cocktail shaker. Shake well for about 30 seconds, then strain into a tall glass over the remaining ice cubes. Float the Galliano on top. Decorate with orange slices and serve with straws.

6 ice cubes

1 measure vodka

125 ml (4 fl oz) fresh orange juice

1–2 teaspoons Galliano

orange slices, to decorate

Serves 1
Preparation time: 3 minutes

A drink from the 1960s, the Harvey Wallbanger is said to have been named after a Californian surfer who drank so much of it that as he found his way out of the bar he banged and bounced from one wall to the other.

hawaiian vodka

4–5 ice cubes
1 measure pineapple juice
juice of 1 lemon
juice of 1 orange
1 teaspoon grenadine
3 measures vodka
lemon slice, to decorate

Put the ice cubes into a cocktail shaker. Pour the pineapple, lemon and orange juices, grenadine and vodka over the ice and shake until a frost forms. Strain into a tumbler and decorate with a slice of lemon. Drink with a straw.

Serves 1

Preparation time: 3 minutes

champagne and wine: bubbly and vino

kir

Put the ice cubes into a goblet or old fashioned glass. Pour the crème de cassis and wine over the ice, stir gently and serve.

Pictured Left

2–3 ice cubes
1 measure crème de cassis
4 measures dry white wine

Serves 1

Preparation time: 3 minutes

Crème de cassis is a blackcurrant-based liqueur from Dijon which blends deliciously with dry white wine. In French bars this drink is sometimes called vin blanc cassis and sometimes kir.

wine cooler

Put the ice cubes into a goblet or tumbler. Pour the elderflower cordial and the wine over the ice then top up with soda water. Decorate with the lemon spiral, stir then serve.

Pictured Right

4–5 ice cubes
1 measure elderflower cordial
4 measures white wine
soda water
lemon spiral, to decorate

Serves 1

Preparation time: 3 minutes

classic champagne cocktail

Put the sugar into a Champagne glass or cocktail glass, and saturate with the bitters. Add the brandy and Cointreau then fill the glass with Champagne. Serve decorated with an orange slice.

1 sugar cube

2–3 drops Angostura bitters

½ teaspoon brandy

½ teaspoon Cointreau

4 measures chilled Champagne

orange slice, to decorate

Serves 1

Preparation time: 2 minutes

If you have time, leave the sugar cubes in the glasses for up to 45 minutes after you have soaked them with the bitters. It will improve the flavour no end.

A splash of Angostura bitters enlivens many cocktails. The pink element in a pink gin, it was first made in the Venezuelan town of Angostura during the nineteenth century but is now produced in Trinidad.

1 tablespoon light rum
1 tablespoon crème de banane
dash of Angostura bitters
chilled Champagne or sparkling wine

To Decorate:
slice of banana
slice of pineapple
cocktail cherry

Pour the rum, crème de banane and bitters into a chilled Champagne flute. Top up with Champagne and stir gently. Decorate with the banana, pineapple and cherry, all speared on a cocktail stick.

Serves 1
Preparation time: 3 minutes

caribbean champagne

millennium cocktail

Put the ice cubes into a cocktail shaker, add the vodka, raspberry and orange juice and shake thoroughly. Strain into a Champagne glass and pour in the chilled Champagne.

4–5 ice cubes

1 measure vodka

1 measure fresh raspberry juice

1 measure fresh orange juice

4 measures Champagne or sparkling dry white wine

Serves 1
Preparation time: 3 minutes

4–5 ice cubes
2 measures vodka
½ measure peach schnapps
1 teaspoon peach juice
Champagne

Serves 1
Preparation time: 3 minutes

Put the ice cubes, vodka, peach schnapps and peach juice into a cocktail shaker and shake thoroughly. Strain into a chilled cocktail glass and top up with Champagne.

bellinitini

non-alcoholic drinks: pussyfoots

prohibition punch

125 ml (4 fl oz) sugar syrup
350 ml (12 fl oz) fresh lemon juice
900 ml (1½ pints) apple juice
ice cubes
2.4 litres (4 pints) ginger ale
orange slices, to decorate

Serves 25–30

Preparation time: 10 minutes

Stir together the sugar syrup, lemon and apple juices in a large chilled jug. Add the ice cubes and pour in the ginger ale. Decorate with orange slices and serve.

carrot cream

Put the carrot juice, cream, egg yolks and orange juice into a cocktail shaker and shake well. Divide the ice cubes among 4 tall glasses and pour the carrot drink on top. Decorate with orange slices and serve immediately. Drink with straws.

250 ml (8 fl oz) carrot juice

300 ml (½ pint) single cream

4 egg yolks

125 ml (4 fl oz) fresh orange juice

20 ice cubes

orange slices, to decorate

Serves 4

Preparation time: 4 minutes

Carrot juice and orange juice blend very well in this delicious and nutritious drink.

grapefruit mint cooler

Put the sugar and water into a heavy-based saucepan and stir over a low heat until dissolved. Leave to cool. Crush the mint leaves and stir them into the syrup. Cover and leave to stand for about 12 hours, then strain into a jug. Add the lemon and grapefruit juices to the strained syrup and stir well. Fill 6 old fashioned glasses or tumblers with crushed ice and pour the cocktail into the glasses. Pour in the soda water and decorate with mint sprigs.

125 g (4 oz) sugar

125 ml (4 fl oz) water

handful of mint sprigs

juice of 4 large lemons

450 ml (¾ pint) fresh grapefruit juice

crushed ice

250 ml (8 fl oz) soda water

mint sprigs, to decorate

Serves 6

Preparation time: 10 minutes, plus standing

To make a Cranberry Mint Cooler, substitute cranberry juice for the grapefruit juice.

3 ice cubes
1 measure fresh orange juice
1 measure fresh lemon juice
1 measure pineapple juice
1 measure fresh grapefruit juice
2 dashes grenadine
1 egg white
soda water

To Decorate:
lemon slice
lime slice
cocktail cherry
orange spiral

Serves 1
Preparation time: 4 minutes

Put the ice cubes into a cocktail shaker and pour in the orange, lemon, pineapple and grapefruit juices, grenadine and egg white. Shake well then strain into a large goblet. Top up with soda water and decorate with the lemon and lime slices and cocktail cherry on a cocktail stick and an orange spiral. Drink through a straw.

san francisco

index

Special Photography:
Neil Mersh
Jacket Photography:
Neil Mersh
Cocktail Preparation:
Ben & Paul
The Salmon & Compasses
58 Penton Street
London
N1 9PZ